SHOW ME THY WAYS

Gertrude Hoeksema

Grade 4

D1606828

Reformed Free
Publishing Association

©1988 Reformed Free Publishing Association
Second Printing 1994
Third Printing 1995
Fourth Printing 2008
Fifth Printing 2018

Printed in the United States of America

Reformed Free Publishing Association
1894 Georgetown Center Drive

Jenison, Michigan 49428

616-457-5970

www.rfpa.org

mail@rfpa.org

ISBN: 0-916206-36-X
LCCN 88-61905

Exercises for Lessons 1 to 3

1. In Lesson 1, we tried to say something about our God. So did Job. He asked a question about finding out about God. Copy the text in Job 11:7, and then answer Job's question.

_____

_____

_____

2. On the Bible next to this question, print the text which tells us, right from the mouth of God, how He gave His Word to men. You will find it in II Timothy 3:16.

3. Do you know that the Psalms tell us that God's creation was formed by the breath of God's mouth? Psalm 33:6 tells us about God's Word of creation. Write the text on these lines.

_____

_____

_____

4. On day one God created _____ . Compare the light of God's creation in Genesis 1:4 with the light of the new heaven and earth in Revelation 22:5. First, carefully read each text. Then, in a complete sentence, tell how the light of the new heaven and earth is greater than the light of God's first creation. _____

_____

5. On day two God created the _____. Psalm 104 is a song of praise to God for His wonderful world. Copy Psalm 104:2 and underline the word which tells what the heavens are like. _____

_____

6. Although we are studying the first book of the Bible, Malachi, the writer of the last book of the Old Testament, wrote about the Sun. Our sun in the heavens is a picture of the Sun that Malachi wrote about. Read Malachi 4:2. Who is the Sun of Righteousness? Write His name on the sun. What does He bring to His people? Write it on the sun.

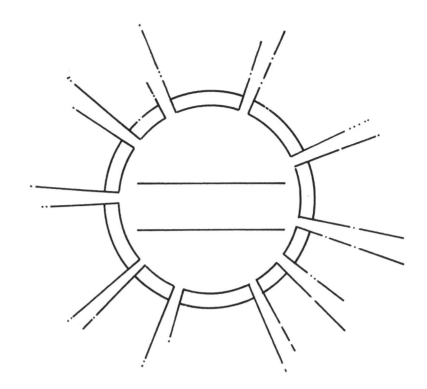

7. Read Psalm 104:13-16. Find at least five things we could stock in our kitchens, and write them on these lines.

_____

_____

_____

_____

_____

IDEA CORNER:

1. Give three or four examples telling how the time which God created rules your life.

_____

_____

_____

_____

_____

_____

_____

2. For your morning song service, sing Psalter number 86 and notice especially stanza one. The words of this song are taken from Psalm 33. Make number 86 your theme song of the week.

Exercises for Lessons 4 to 6

Match the numbers of the questions on this page to the correct answers on the opposite page.

1. The belief that lower kinds of animals developed into higher kinds, all by themselves, is called: (put a numeral 1 next to the correct answer)

2. On days 5 and 6 God created the living souls. Which living souls are the most unlike man? (put a numeral 2 next to the correct answer)

3. What are the 3 kinds of land animals God created on day six? (put number 3 on 3 answers)

4. Leviticus 17:11 tells us that the life (or soul) of an animal is in its:

5. God created Adam in His:

6. In Paradise, Adam was God's:

7. The seventh day of creation was a picture of the perfect rest of:

8. What was the name of the tree Adam and Eve might not eat of?

9. Whom did the devil tempt first?

10. Adam and Eve died spiritually, in their hearts, because "to live apart from God is. . ."

Turn to Revelation 22:1-5 and find three things which God promises in His heavenly Paradise. Write them on the lines below.

1. _____
_____

2. _____
_____

3. _____
_____

Discuss in class what it must have been like to live in a sinless garden, without death. Did plants ever rot? Did trees drop their leaves and get new ones? Did the animals fight?

heaven

Eve

friend-servant

knowledge of good and evil

evolutionism

image

blood

cattle

death

wild beasts

creeping things

fish

4

Exercises for Lessons 7 to 9

1. On the chart on the opposite page, color the bars of the descendants of Adam. One bar runs through Seth and one bar runs through Cain. Use pencil crayons lightly, and color the bar for each name. Use the same colors for Seth and Cain (for example red), for Enos and Enoch (for example brown), Cainan and Irad, through Enoch and Lamech, the seventh from Adam. Then match the colors of Methuselah, Lamech, and Noah to the three sons of Lamech in the slanting triangles. Now you can see how the lifetimes of the two lines on the earth match one another.

2. In a complete sentence explain why Enoch (in the line of Seth has a line so much shorter than the others. _____

_____

_____

_____

_____

3. If you were Methuselah, could you have asked Adam a question? That is, was Adam still living? _____

4. What question would you have liked to ask Adam?_____

_____

_____

_____

_____

_____

5. Read Matthew 11:25, 26. These are the words of our Lord Jesus. If Jesus was talking about the people in Lesson 8 (and He was), whose line would be the line of the wise and prudent?
_____ Whose line would be the line of the babes?_____

6. Enoch walked with God. Think how you walk with God. In a short paragraph, in complete sentences, describe what it means for you to walk with God. You may want to tell what is easier and what is harder for you to do when you walk with God.

_____

_____

_____

_____

_____

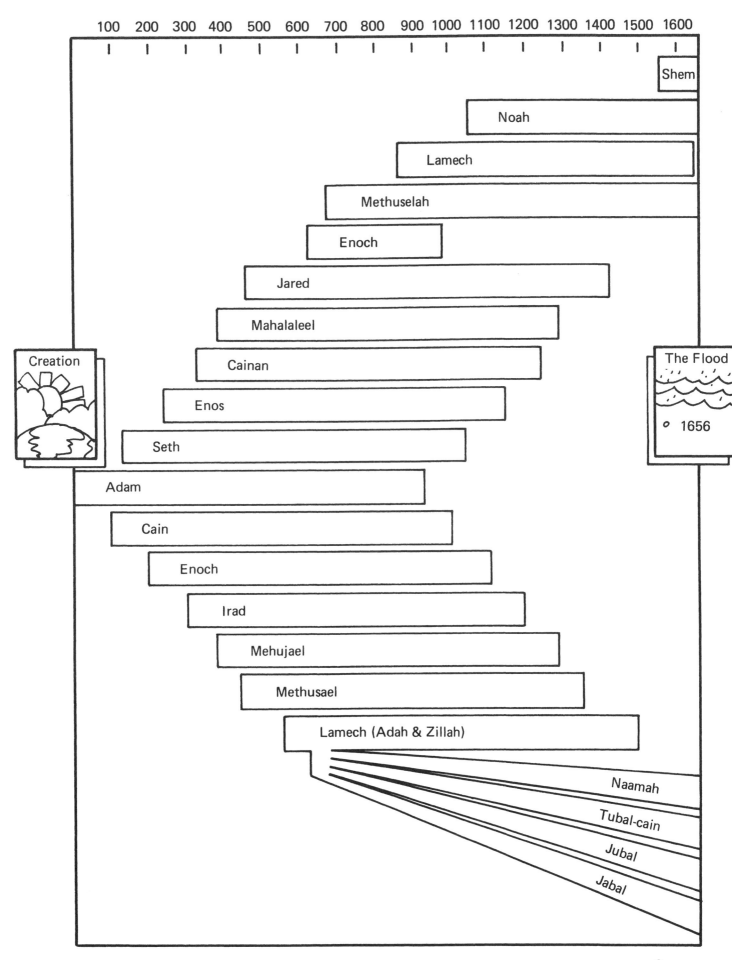

100 200 300 400 500 600 700 800 900 1000 1100 1200 1300 1400 1500 1600

Shem

Noah

Lamech

Methuselah

Enoch

Jared

Mahalaleel

Cainan

Enos

Seth

Creation

Adam

Cain

Enoch

Irad

Mehujael

Methusael

Lamech (Adah & Zillah)

The Flood

1656

Naamah

Tubal-cain

Jubal

Jabal

6

On each ray of the rainbow, print the answers to the following questions.

You may use your textbooks.

1. How many days did the water stay on the earth before the ark came to rest?

2. How long did it take before the tops of the mountains could be seen?

3. How many days later did Noah send out his raven?

4. How many days later did Noah send out a dove?

5. How many days later did Noah send out a second dove?

6. How many days later did Noah send out a third dove?

7. How many months later did Noah and his family leave the ark?

They had been in the ark for _____

Now color the rainbow with your pencil crayons.

An easy way to remember its colors is by the name ROY G. BIV.

It stands for Red, Orange, Yellow, Green, Blue, Indigo, Violet.

(Indigo is a deep violet blue.)

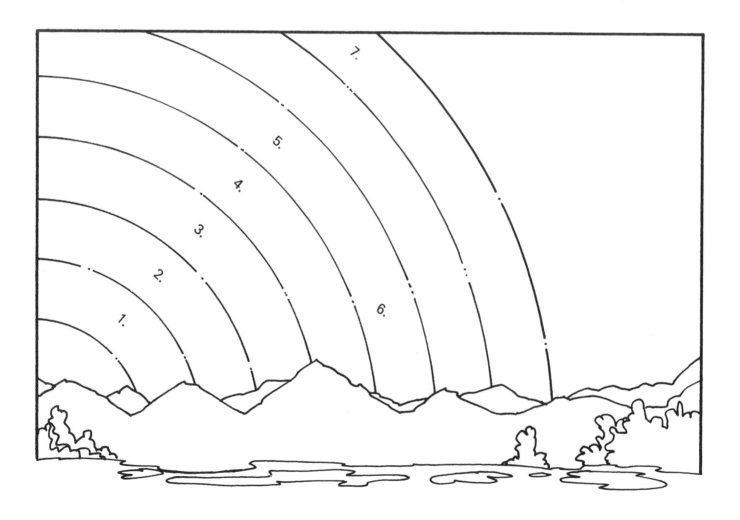

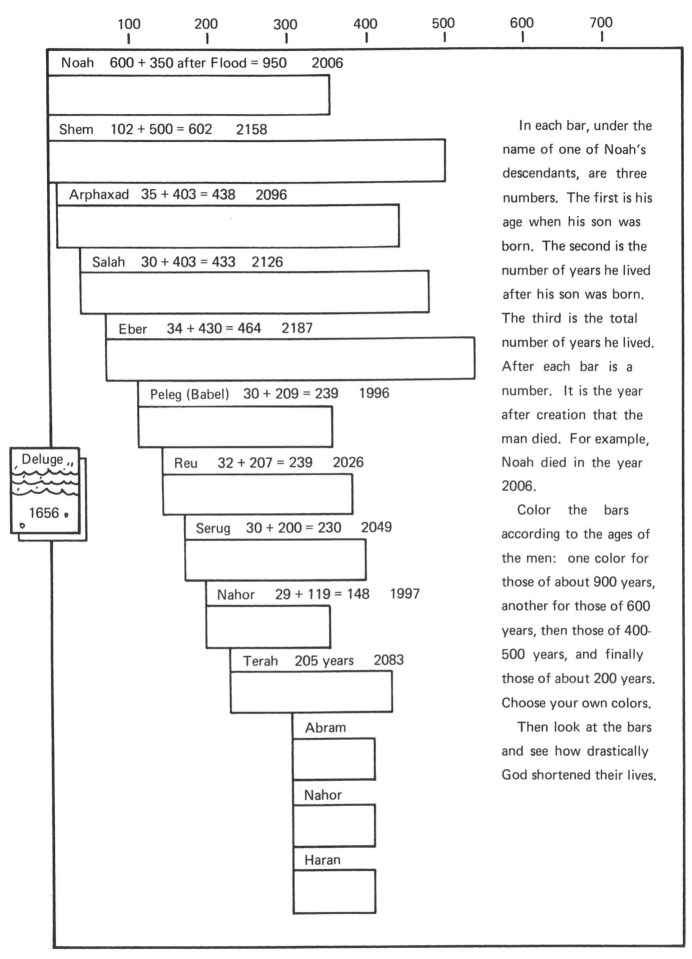

100 200 300 400 500 600 700

Noah   600 + 350 after Flood = 950   2006

Shem   102 + 500 = 602   2158

Arphaxad   35 + 403 = 438   2096

Salah   30 + 403 = 433   2126

Eber   34 + 430 = 464   2187

Peleg (Babel)   30 + 209 = 239   1996

Deluge

1656

Reu   32 + 207 = 239   2026

Serug   30 + 200 = 230   2049

Nahor   29 + 119 = 148   1997

Terah   205 years   2083

Abram

Nahor

Haran

In each bar, under the name of one of Noah's descendants, are three numbers. The first is his age when his son was born. The second is the number of years he lived after his son was born. The third is the total number of years he lived. After each bar is a number. It is the year after creation that the man died. For example, Noah died in the year 2006.

Color the bars according to the ages of the men: one color for those of about 900 years, another for those of 600 years, then those of 400-500 years, and finally those of about 200 years. Choose your own colors.

Then look at the bars and see how drastically God shortened their lives.

8

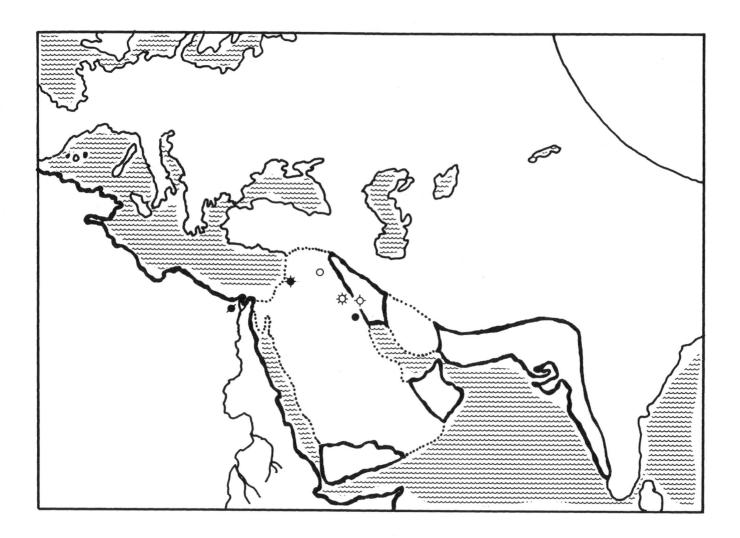

1. Print Shinar next to the ◇ . (The whole area was the Plain of Shinar.)

2. Print Babel next to the ☼ .

3. Print Ur next to the ● .

4. Print Haran next to the ○ .

5. Print Canaan next to the ✦ .

6. Print Egypt next to the ✺ .

7. Follow the coloring instructions very carefully. Using pencil crayons:

   Color the pieces of land bordered with heavy lines yellow. Ham's descendants lived in these lands. ▬▬▬▬

   Color the pieces of land bordered with dotted lines green. Shem's descendants lived in these lands. ••••••••••••

   Color the rest of the land, outlined in lighter lines, a pale red or purple. Japheth's descendants lived in these lands. ▬▬▬▬

   Color the seas and rivers light blue.

Now you can see how God scattered the descendants of Noah.

9

1. Print Tigris next to the ⬦ .

2. Print Euphrates next to the ☼ .

These rivers come together near Ur.

3. Print Ur next to the ● .

4. Print Babylon (a later name for Babel) next to the ○ .

5. Print Haran next to the ✦ .

6. Print Shechem next to the ✺ .

7. Print Bethel next to the ✦ .

8. Print Egypt next to the ✐ .

9. Print Hebron next to the △ .

    With pencil, trace Abram's journey from Ur to Babylon, to Haran, to Shechem, to Bethel, to Egypt, back to Bethel, to Hebron.

    With pencil crayon, color all the land area one color. You may choose the color. Color the seas and trace the rivers in blue.

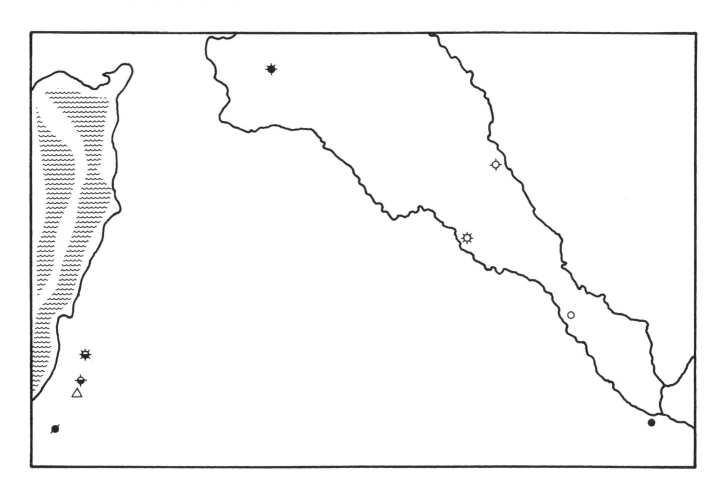

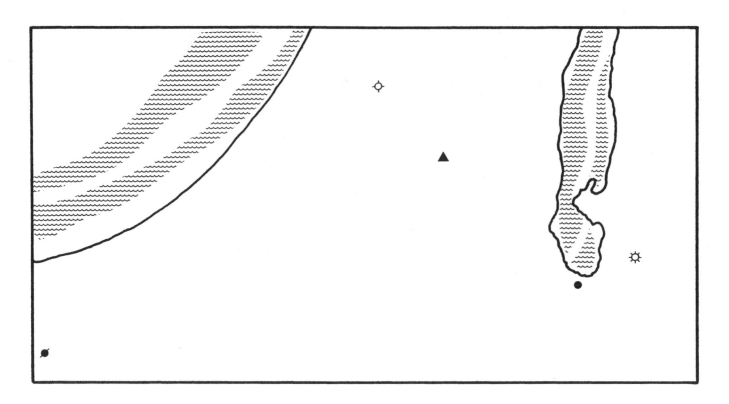

On this map of the southern part of the land of Canaan,

the history of our last three lessons took place.

1. Print Shur next to the ✹ . Who fled to Shur? _____

2. Print Hebron next to the ✧ .

3. Print Plains of Mamre next to the ▲ . Who lived on the Plains of Mamre? _____

4. Print Sodom and Gomorrah next to the ✡ .

5. Print Zoar next to the ● . Why is Zoar important? _____

_____

6. Print Dead Sea in the body of water.

7. With pencil crayons, color all the land one color.

SOME OF YOUR OWN THOUGHTS

Read Hebrews 13:1, 2, and think about it. Abraham did what God tells us to do in these verses. Write two or three sentences about the way you let brotherly love continue in your life.

_____

_____

_____

_____

_____

THIS IS A REVIEW OF SOME OF THE WORDS WE LEARNED
IN OUR FIRST SIX WEEKS

Circle the correct answer (or answers).

1. God's revelation is (2 answers)

   what He told us about Himself   the beginning of the world   the Bible

2. The theory of evolutionism teaches that (2 answers)

   our world is small   our world happened by chance

   our world developed over millions of years

3. The universe is

   the light God created   the beaten-out firmament

   the whole system of things God created

4. Subtle means

   clever   sinful   quick

5. The seed of the serpent is

   a snake   the ungodly in the world   the human race

6. A genealogy is

   a map   a history of the lines of a family   a judgment on the world

7. Oral tradition is

   the number of years a man lived   the way people lived

   the way the Word of God was passed from one generation to the next

8. God's covenant with His people is (2 answers)

   an agreement   a relation of friendship   a promise

9. A Hebrew means

   from the other side   a messenger   a protection

10. Tithes are (2 answers)

    gifts   a tenth part   priests

11. When Abraham was hospitable, he was

    eager to serve   sick   worried about Lot

12. Brimstone is

    gold   fire   sulfur

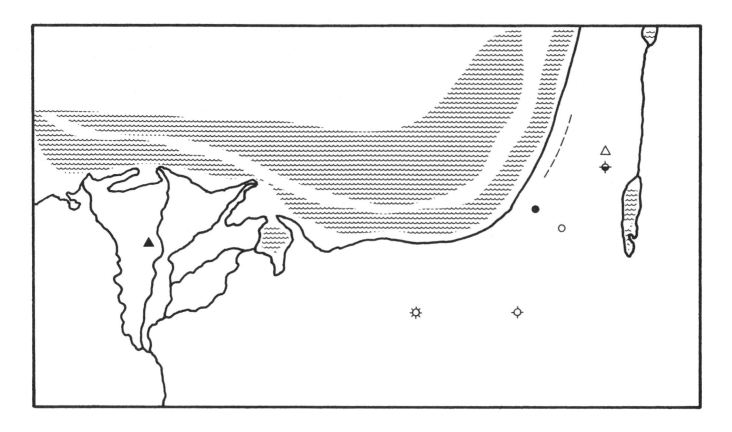

To learn about the later part of Abraham's life,

we will find the places he visited.

1. Print Kadesh next to the ✧ and Shur next to the ☼ .

2. Print Gerar next to the ● . Who was king of Gerar? _____

3. Print Philistia on the dotted line.

4. In Lesson 19, we learned that Mizraim was one of the sons of Ham. He settled in Egypt. Sometimes the Bible calls Egypt Mizraim. Print Mizraim next to the ▲ . Put Egypt in parentheses under it.

5. Print Beersheba next to the ○ . Who wandered in the wilderness of Beersheba?_____

6. Print Salem next to the ✦ . Salem was later called Jerusalem. Mt. Moriah was the mountain on which the temple at Jerusalem was later built.

7. Print Mt. Moriah next to the △ . In a complete sentence, tell what great event took place at Mt. Moriah. _____

_____

_____

8. Color the map the colors you wish.

After the Bible has given us so much history and so many stories about Abraham, we feel as if we know Abraham and his family and friends quite well; and that is the way God wants it to be. He wants us to know and understand the revelation He has given us.

You will see the names of six people we have studied this week. Behind each name are blanks, in which you will write two different sets of words which describe them. You may pretend you are describing them for someone who does not know them. I will give you a start.

1. Sarah   a mother at ninety _____   _____

2. Abraham   _____   _____

3. Isaac   _____   _____

4. Ishmael   _____   _____

5. Hagar   _____   _____

6. Abimelech   _____   _____

The Bible interprets itself. Do you know what that means? It means that other parts of the Bible explain the chapters we are studying, to help us understand our lesson better.

1. Galatians 4 tells about Hagar and Sarah. Read verse 22, and tell which word describes Hagar _____ , and which word describes Sarah _____ .

2. Now read verse 31. That verse tells us that we are children of _____

_____

_____

_____

FOR EXTRA CREDIT

Abraham was obedient, faithful, and God's friend. Think for a while, and then in a short paragraph, write the name you would like to be called by the Lord. It must describe what lives in your heart. Then tell why you chose that name.

_____

_____

_____

_____

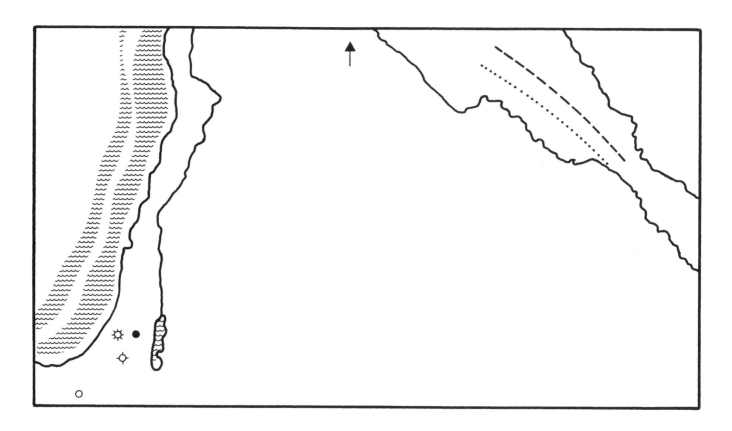

We will be using this map for next week's lessons, too.

1. Print Beersheba next to the ✧ .

2. Print Kirjath-Arba next to the ☼ . Kirjath-Arba is another name for the city of _____ (Lesson 22).

3. Print Machpelah next to the ● . Who was buried in the cave of Machpelah? _____

4. Print Haran next to the ↑ . Haran was also called the city of Nahor, who was Abraham's

_____ .

5. Print Mesopotamia on the line with dashes (---------). Often the Bible uses another name, Padan Aram. **Print** Padan Aram underneath, on the dotted line.

6. Print Lahai-roi next to the ○ . It was the well that Hagar named. What does Lahai-roi mean? _____

REVIEW

1. In Lesson 22 we learned that Abraham told his servant that the Lord would sent His angel before him when he went to get a wife for Isaac. The Bible tells us much about angels. Matthew 18:10 tells us that the angels take care of "these little ones." Who do you think these little ones are? _____

_____

_____

_____

_____

2. Matthew 24:31 tells us about the angels and the end of the world. What instrument will the angels play then? _____

3. You will remember that when Eliezer, Abraham's servant, prayed to the Lord at the well, the Lord answered him before he had finished speaking. Do you know that the Lord promises that to us, too? Find Isaiah 65:24, and write it on these lines. _____

_____

_____

_____

_____

This is a special promise of God to us, and it is a text you all will want to memorize.

4. On the basis of this chart, what relation was Rebekah to Isaac?

BROTHERS	Abraham	Nahor	Haran (died)
SONS	Isaac	Bethuel	Lot
DAUGHTER		Rebekah	

Answer: _____

5. In Lesson 24 we learned two long words: election (those whom God chose to be saved) and reprobation (those whom God rejected). Do you know when God chose His people to be His own? Turn to Ephesians 1:4 and find the six words which tell us.

_____   _____

_____   _____

_____   _____

In one or two sentences, tell what makes you most happy that you are one. _____

_____

_____

_____

_____

In our lessons so far this year, we have learned very much about God's promises to His people. We call it God's revelation to them. He told them about it, very simply at first. Slowly He added more details of His covenant promises of friendship. Because we have the whole Bible, we know that all these promises lead to the coming of our Lord Jesus, and His sacrifice for our sins. But Abraham, Isaac, and Jacob could not see those promises so clearly as we can.

We will review some of those promises in this worksheet.

1. In Genesis 12:2, God gave a simple promise to Abram. He said, "And I will make of thee

_____ , and I will _____ ."

2. In Genesis 15:5, God told Abram how great the nation would be. He asked Abram to look toward _____ and count the _____ and He ended the verse by saying, "So _____ ."

3. In Genesis 17:8, God told Abraham what land He would give him. It would be all _____

_____ .

4. In Genesis 18:10, God told Abraham how He would give him this land of Canaan. He said to this old man, "and, lo, _____

_____

_____ .

5. In Genesis 22:18 God promised Abraham much more than the land of Canaan. Copy the whole verse on these lines, and then memorize it. This is a beautiful verse to keep in your heart.

_____

_____

_____

_____

_____

In this puzzle, which spells JACOB COMES TO BETHEL,

fit in the answers with the letter which is given.

1. Who gave Jacob a promise at Bethel?
2. What was the name of Jacob's uncle, to whom he fled?
3. Who is the son who tricked his father?
4. On what did Jacob pour oil at Bethel?
5. Name the city where Isaac dug his last well, Genesis 26:33.
6. Who was a blind old man?
7. Name the well which means "the Lord has made room for us."
8. Whose name means "my father is king?"
9. What did Jacob have the night he slept at Bethel?
10. Which brother had murder in his heart?
11. Name the well whose name means "enmity" or "hatred."
12. What skins did Rebekah put on Jacob's hands?
13. Name the woman who listened at Isaac's tent.
14. Name the well whose name means "contention" or argument."
15. Name the place which means "house of God."
16. To what place did Jacob flee?
17. To what city did Isaac go in the time of famine?
18. Who walked up and down the ladder in Jacob's dream?

J _ _ _ _ _ _   _ _ T _ _ _

_ A _ _ _   _ O _ _ _

_ _ C _ _   _ _ B _ _ _ _

_ _ O _ _   E _ _ _

B _ _ _ _ _ _ _   _ _ T _ _ _

_ _ _ _ C   H _ _ _ _

_ _ _ O _ _ _ _   _ E _ _ _

_ _ _ M _ _ _ _ _   _ _ _ _ L _

_ _ E _ _

_ S _ _

Jacob really had four wives: Rachel and Leah and their two maids, Bilhah and Zilpah. Although God's law allowed Jacob only one wife, he went his own way and married two wives, plus their maids. And the Lord let him go, although He brought him much trouble later in his life because of this disobedience. The sons from these marriages became the heads of the tribes of Israel. To make it easier for you to understand, you will work with the figure of a tree on the opposite page.

1. We may say that because God called Abraham first, he was the root. Print Abraham next to the 1.

2. Print Isaac next to the 2. We may say that he was the continuing line, or the trunk.

3. Print Jacob next to the 3, near the top of the trunk, for in Jacob God branched out His children.

4. Print Leah next to the 4 on the main branch. She was the important covenant mother.

5. Print Rachel next to the 5.

6. Print Bilhah next to the 6.

7. Print Zilpah next to the 7.

8. Print the names of Leah's children in the order of their ages. Print Reuben on the bottom branch, and move up the branch with the following names: Simeon, Levi, Judah, Issachar, and Zebulon.

9. Print Joseph and Benjamin on Rachel's branch. In our lessons for this week, Benjamin has not been born yet.

10. Print Dan and Naphtali on Bilhah's branch.

11. Print Gad and Asher on Zilpah's branch.

12. Outline the tree in color.

Exercises for Lessons 31 to 33

On the map of the land of Canaan on the opposite page, we will name the places where Jacob and his sons lived, and trace some of their journeys.

1. Print Jabbok River next to the ▲ .
2. Print Jordan River next to the △ .
3. Print Succoth next to the ⬦ .
4. What did Jacob build for himself at Succoth? _____
5. Print Shechem next to the ☼ .
6. Print Bethel next to the ● .
7. What did Jacob do at Bethel? _____
8. Print Ramah next to the ○ .
9. What happened at Ramah? _____
10. Print Mamre next to the ✦ .
11. Draw a line from Succoth through Shechem and all the places Jacob traveled until he came to Mamre.
12. Print Seir next to the ✹ . Another name for Seir is _____ .
13. Print Dothan next to the ◆ .
14. Print Egypt next to the arrow. It is not on this map.
15. Trace Joseph's journey from Mamre, north to Shechem, to Dothan, and south again to the arrow pointing to Egypt, with broken lines like this: -------. That is Joseph's journey to Egypt.

IDEA CORNER

Make Psalter number 121:2 (taken from Psalm 44) your song for the week. It tells that Jacob and his sons could not capture the land of Canaan. It was all God's work.

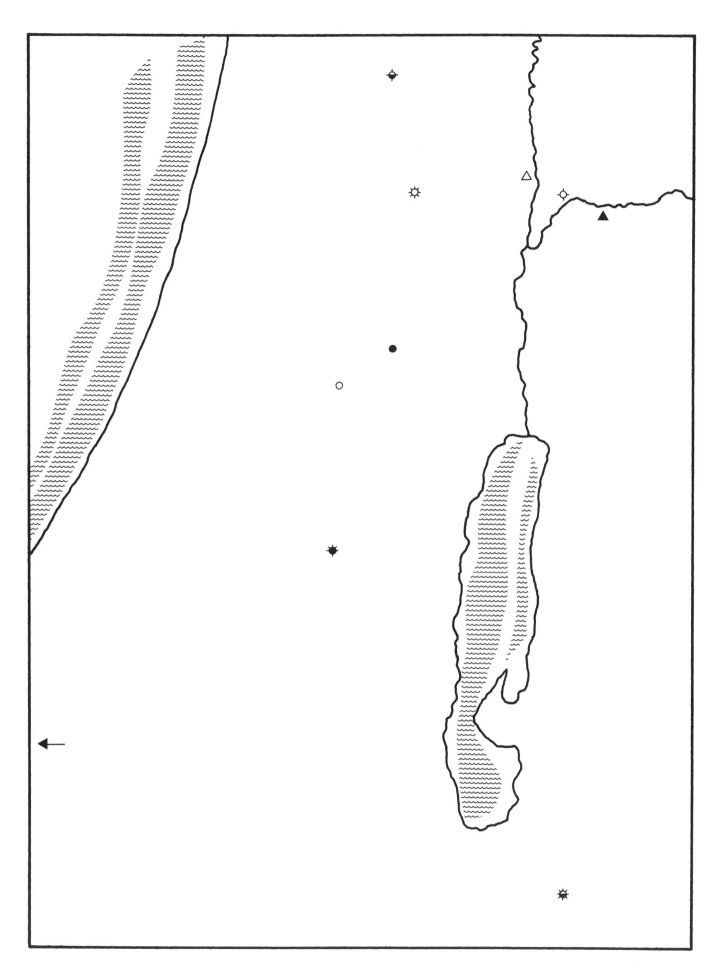

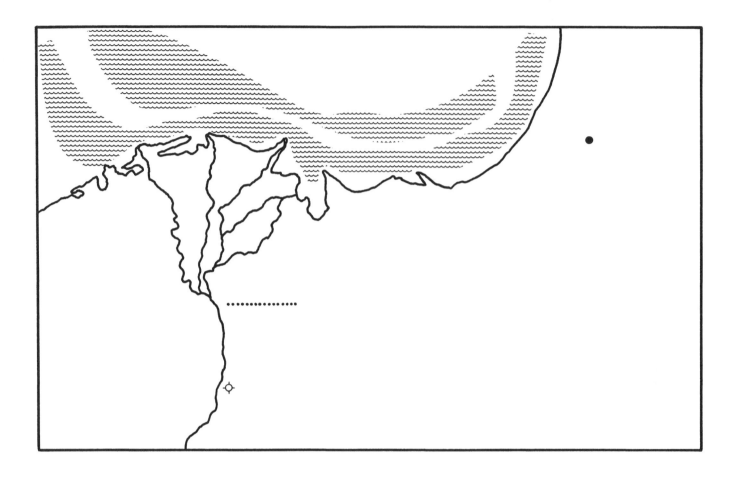

This is a small map of Canaan and Egypt. Follow the directions below.

1. Print Egypt on the dotted line.
2. Print Nile next to the ✧ .
3. Who dreamed about the River Nile? _____
4. Print Hebron next to the ● .
5. Draw a line from Hebron to Egypt.
6. Who traveled this route to Egypt? _____

Try to solve this problem: If Joseph collected 10,000 bushels of grain in a day, and saved a fifth part of the grain for the storehouse cities, how many bushels did his servants have to store each day?

WORD MATCHING

We have finished another six weeks of lessons. We found the meanings for these words in our lessons. On the dotted line next to each word, put the number of the right answer below.

1. integrity ____	1. storekeepers
2. rebellious ____	2. disobey authority
3. persecute ____	3. wise
4. veil ____	4. those who are rejected by God
5. meditating ____	5. beg
6. entreat ____	6. covering for a face
7. elect people ____	7. ungodly
8. reprobate people ____	8. honesty
9. profane ____	9. house of God
10. Bethel ____	10. to fortell the future
11. merchantmen ____	11. manager
12. discreet ____	12. to treat with cruel hatred
13. steward ____	13. those who are chosen by God
14. to divine ____	14. thinking or praying

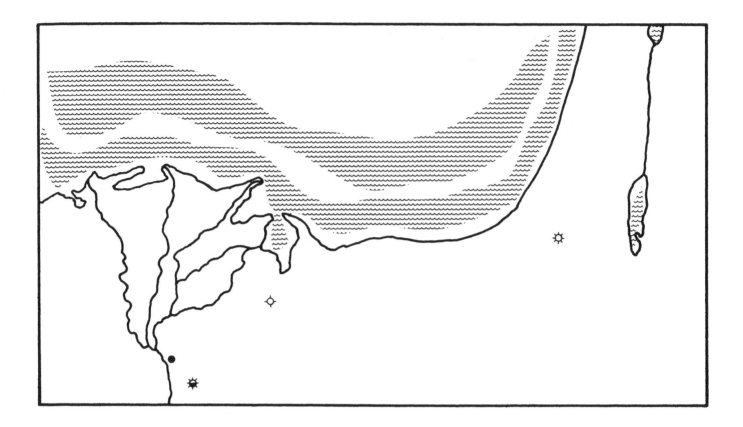

MAP WORK

1. Next to the ☼ draw a small altar and print Beersheba under it. Who built an altar at

Beersheba? _____

2. Next to the ♦ draw a picture of one of the kinds of animals Jacob's family had in Goshen.

Under the picture, print Goshen.

3. Print Nile River next to the ● .

4. Print Egypt next to the ☀ .

IDEA CORNER

In Genesis 49:22 and 23, Jacob gave two different pictures of Joseph. Read both verses

carefully and choose one. On a separate sheet of paper draw a picture of the words of Jacob in

the verse you choose.

1. Judah was the son from whose line Jesus would be born. God, through Jacob's mouth, made word pictures of Judah which are pictures of Jesus.

    a. First, copy Genesis 49:9 on these lines and underline lion in the text. _____

_____

_____

_____

_____

    b. Now find Revelation 5:5 and see how God made Jacob's prophecy come true. Underline lion again. _____

_____

_____

_____

_____

2. A sceptre is the staff of a king. You will find the word in verse 10. Shiloh means peace and is a name of Jesus.

    a. Copy Genesis 49:10 and underline sceptre. _____

_____

_____

_____

_____

    b. Find Hebrews 1:8 and copy it and underline sceptre. _____

_____

_____

_____

_____

Match the following, using chapter 49 in your Bibles.

1. Dan   instruments of cruelty

2. Zebulon   haven of the sea

3. Issachar   royal dainties

4. Benjamin   a strong ass

5. Simeon and Levi   a serpent

6. Asher   a wolf

IDEA CORNER

    Look up embalming practices in an encyclopedia. Find pictures and discuss it in class.

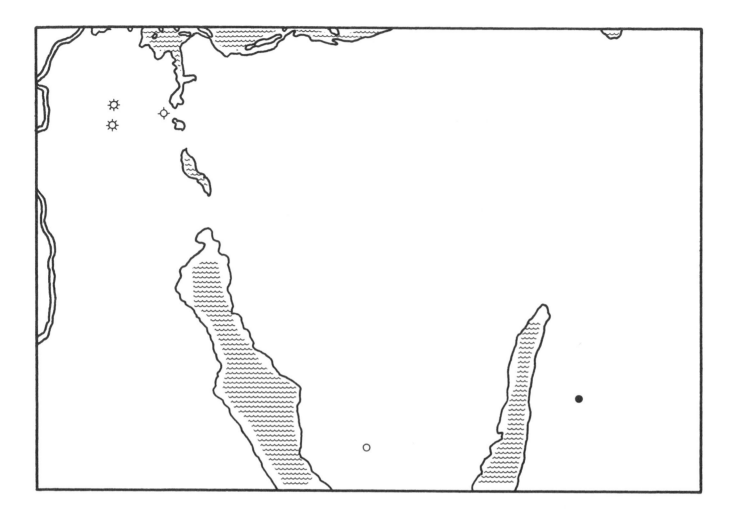

MAP WORK

1. Print Goshen next to the ✧ .

2. Print Pithom and Raamses next to the ☼ .

3. What were Pithom and Raamses? _____

4. Print Midian next to the ● .

5. With whom did Moses live in Midian? _____

6. Whom did Moses marry? _____

7. Print Horeb next to the ○ . Horeb was a group of mountains. One of the peaks was called
Mount Sinai. It was also called the Mount of God. We will visit that peak with the Israelites later
in our lessons. Who met Moses at the Mount of God? _____

1. The main idea of our three lessons this week was that the Lord used the wicked Pharaoh to bring the children of Israel so much suffering that they begged Him to take them out of Egypt. God's purpose in doing all this work in Egypt was that He will have all the glory.

Romans 9:17 is one verse from the Bible which tells us this beautiful truth. Write it on these lines and think about it and remember it. _____

_____

_____

_____

_____

In this text God wanted to show two reasons why He raised up Pharaoh. Underline the first reason in blue pencil crayon and the second reason in orange.

2. We learned, too, that the devil worked through Pharaoh to hurt and destroy God's people. It will be interesting to see how often the devil did this. Find the following texts, read each one carefully, and write in your own words what the devil was doing through Pharaoh's cruel rules. I will help you with the first one.

a. Read Exodus 1:11 — The taskmasters made them carry heavy burdens when they built the two treasure cities. _____

b. Read Exodus 1:14 — _____

_____

c. Read Exodus 1:16 (the last part, starting with the word if) — _____

_____

d. Read Exodus 1:22 — _____

_____

e. Read Exodus 5:7 — _____

_____

_____

Ten is God's number of fulness, of completeness. He sent ten plagues. Nine would not have been enough. Eleven would have been too many. The ten plagues filled the measure of Egypt's wickedness. After the tenth plague the Lord was ready to judge them, especially Pharaoh, who would not obey Him.

In this cup of God's anger, we will start the plagues with the first one at the bottom and the tenth plague filling the measure of God's judgment.

1. Print the name of each plague in the cup. Look ahead to Exodus 11:5 for the tenth plague.

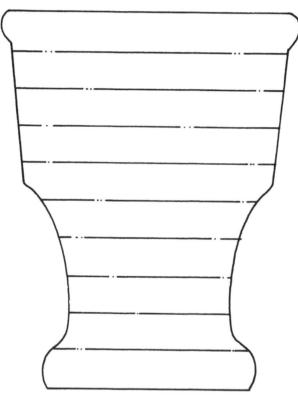

2. What truth about Egypt's gods did God show in the first group of plagues? See the DO NOT FORGET in Lesson 43. _____

_____

3. What truth about Himself did God show in the second group of plagues? See the BEFORE WE BEGIN in Lesson 44. _____

_____

4. What truth about Himself did God show in the third group of plagues? See LESSON OUTLINE — A — 1 in Lesson 45. _____

_____

The time of the plagues and the time of Israel leaving Egypt is a very important period in Bible history. Often later writers of the Bible look back to this period and teach us more about it. As we do this worksheet, we will learn why the Bible teaches us about it.

1. Do you know the names of two of Pharaoh's magicians? Paul wrote about them in his second letter to Timothy. Find their names in II Timothy 3:8, and write them on these lines:

_____   _____

On the next line write what kind of men they were. _____

_____

2. Asaph, the song-writer, wrote about God's wonders in Egypt. Psalms 78 and 105 give us more details about the plagues. In these Psalms God shows how dreadful it was to live through those judgments, and he shows how the people suffered.

   a. Everyone suffered. Not even Pharaoh escaped. Find Psalm 105:30 and tell one of the places the frogs came. _____

   b. Read Psalm 78:46. Notice the word increase. That is the people's wages, their money. Now notice the word labor. It means their hard work. In a sentence, tell what happened to all the people's riches and hard work. _____

_____

_____

_____

   c. Both Psalms 78 and 105 add some details to the plague of the hail storm. Find three details in Psalm 78:47, 48:   _____

_____   _____

   Add two more details from Psalm 105:32: _____

_____

   d. Read Psalm 78:49. Who were the evil angels God sent to Egypt? _____

_____

Exercises for Lessons 46 to 48

MAP WORK

On this map you will follow the journey of the Israelites out of Egypt to Rephidim.

1. Print Raamses next to the ✧ .
2. Print Succoth next to the ☼ .
3. Print Etham next to the ● .
4. Print Pihahiroth next to the ○ .
5. Print Baalzephon next to the ✦ .
6. Print Marah next to the ✷ .
7. Print Elim next to the ✦ .
8. Print Wilderness of Sin on the dotted line.
9. Print Rephidim next to the ✿ .
10. Print Sinai Peninsula on the broken line.
11. Print Red Sea next to the ▲ .
12. Print Wilderness of Shur on the line.
13. Print Gulf of Suez sideways in the body of water next to the △ .
14. Print Gulf of Akaba sideways in the body of water next to the □ .

Show the travels of the Israelites by drawing a line from Raamses through each number to Rephidim.

Color the map. Use a light tan for the wilderness.

IDEA CORNER

The Pillar of Cloud by day and the Pillar of Fire by night was the Leader of the Israelites. We just learned that it was also a type of Christ, the Angel of God's presence. He was the Strength they needed in the frightening wilderness. Psalter number 392, from Psalm 144, has beautiful words about God as the Rock and Helper of His people. Make stanzas 1 and 5 your theme song for the week.

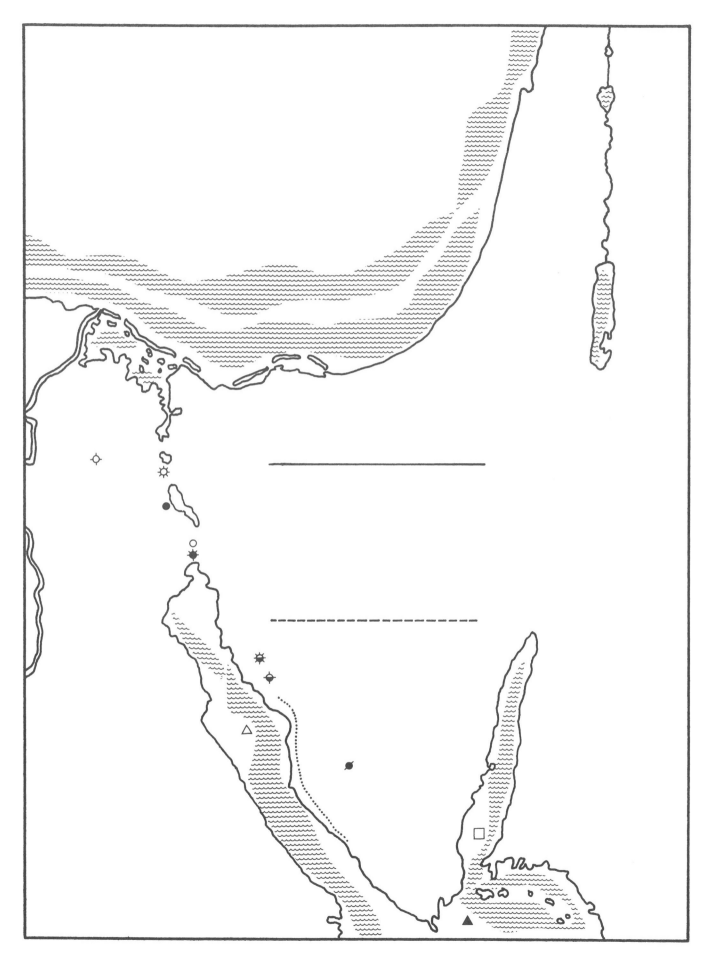

Exercises for Lessons 49 to 51

Now that we have finished one semester of studying God's care over His people in Old Testament times, it is appropriate that we remember His care for us. On this worksheet we will write two short paragraphs.

Remember the truths about God which you have learned and tell how they fit into your life. 1. The Israelites hungered and thirsted after food and water. It was a type of their hunger and thirst for spiritual food, the bread and water of life. In a short paragraph, tell how you hunger and thirst for the bread and water of life.

_____
_____
_____
_____

2. In this paragraph, write why you are glad that Jehovah is your Banner.

_____
_____
_____

IDEA CORNER

This is a short, rhymed version of the ten commandments. It may be sung to the tune of "Praise God, From Whom All Blessings Flow."

1. There is no other God but Me.
   Before no idol bow the knee;
   Take not the name of God in vain,
   Nor dare the sabbath day profane.

2. Give both thy parents honor due,
   Take heed that thou no murder do,
   Abstain from words and deeds unclean;
   Nor steal, though thou be poor and mean.

3. Nor make a wilful lie, nor love it;
   What is thy neighbor's, dare not covet.
   These ten commandments God gave you
   To show His will in all you do.

33

These are the special words, with their meanings, which we learned and used in Lessons 37 to 51. On the line next to each word in the first column, write the numeral of the correct answer in the second column.

1. posterity ____	1. to have good use of language
2. symbol ____	2. to be responsible for someone
3. pilgrim ____	3. many people going away from a country
4. bondage ____	4. descendants, future generations
5. exodus ____	5. a law
6. reproach ____	6. one who journeys to another land
7. sceptre ____	7. to blame or disgrace someone
8. redeem ____	8. contagious disease of cattle
9. surety ____	9. anything that is disgusting or hateful
10. abomination ____	10. a rod which is a sign of power
11. snare ____	11. a sign or a picture
12. murrain ____	12. to set free
13. eloquent ____	13. forced slavery
14. statute ____	14. a trap
15. banner ____	15. a flag or standard of an army

On the opposite page is a sketch of the tabernacle. This will help you understand what the tabernacle looked like, and it will help you understand what each part of the tabernacle means.

PART 1. The dimensions of the tabernacle

    a. On the line at the top of the courtyard, print 150 feet.

       On the side of the courtyard, print 75 feet.

       The walls were 7½ feet high.

    b. Print 45 feet on the long side of the tabernacle and 15 feet on the short side of the tabernacle.

    c. The holy of holies (or most holy place) was 15 feet square. How long was the holy place?

_____

PART 2. After studying Lesson 52, you will be able to recognize the furniture of the tabernacle. Find the following:

    a. Put a b next to the altar of burnt offering.

    b. Put an l next to the laver.

    c. Put an i next to the altar of incense.

    d. Put a t next to the table of showbread.

    e. Put a c next to the lampstand.

    f. Put an a next to the ark of the covenant.

PART 3. Each piece of furniture pointed to the coming of Jesus.

    a. Tell why the Israelites brought animals to the altar of burnt offering. _____

    _____

    b. Of what was the altar of incense a picture?_____

    _____

    c. What did the loaves of bread on the table of showbread mean?_____

    _____

    d. Of what was the candlestick a picture?_____

    _____

    e. Why did the high priest sprinkle blood on the mercy seat in the holy of holies? _____

    _____

IDEA CORNER

To get an idea of the size of the tabernacle, try to measure its size on the playground.

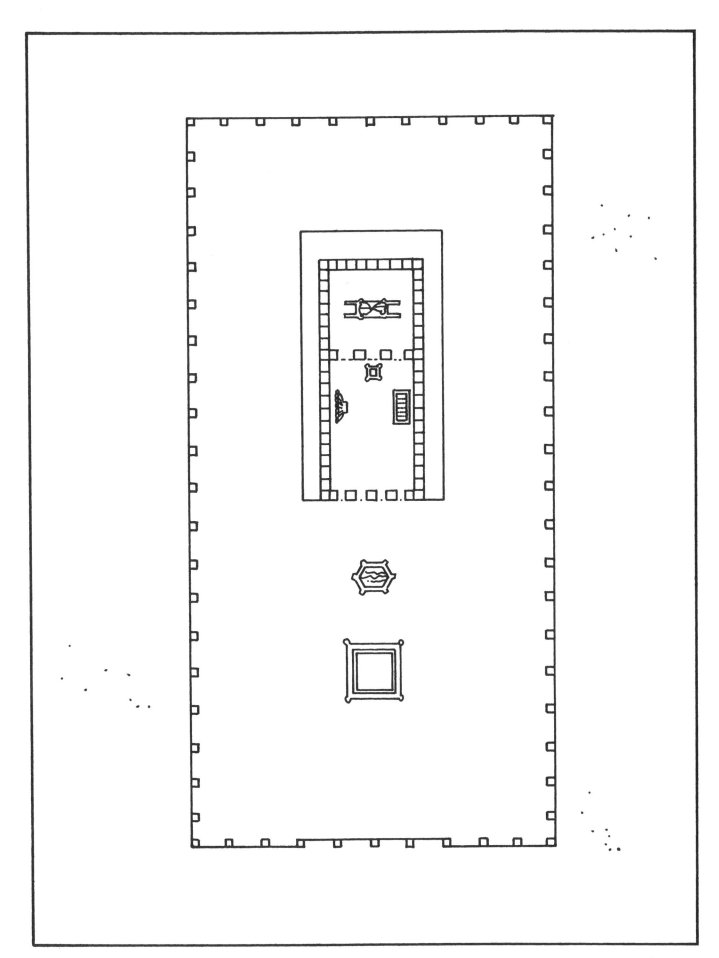

Exercises for Lessons 55 to 57

The Camping Orders

1. On the opposite page you will find a diagram of the camp of Israel as they camped each night according to the Lord's instructions in Numbers 2 and 3. The tabernacle was always in the center of the encampment and always faced east. Print tabernacle on the line under the rectangle.

2. Because they had charge of all the work of the tabernacle, God ordered the Levites to camp on its four sides, close to the tabernacle. The tribe of Levi was divided into four families. Each family had its own side and its own duties.

    a. On the east side, close to the tabernacle, print Moses, Aaron, and sons.

    b. On the south side, print Kohathites.

    c. On the west side, print Gershonites.

    d. On the north side, print Merarites.

3. The twelve tribes of Israel camped on the outside, in groups of three, with one tribe on each side carrying the banner of the leader.

    a. On the banner on the east side, print Judah. On each side of Judah, print Issachar and Zebulon.

    b. On the banner on the south side, print Reuben. On each side, print Simeon and Gad.

    c. On the banner on the west side, print Ephraim. On each side, print Manasseh and Benjamin.

    d. On the banner on the north side, print Dan. On each side, print Asher and Naphtali.

4. When Moses gave the orders to march, the Israelites stayed in the same order. The Bible does not tell us whether they marched in lines or in groups. Sometimes, due to dangers and hardships in the desert, the order of the tribes may have become mixed up. But each night, when Moses spoke the words of Numbers 10:35, the people of Israel came together in an orderly encampment.

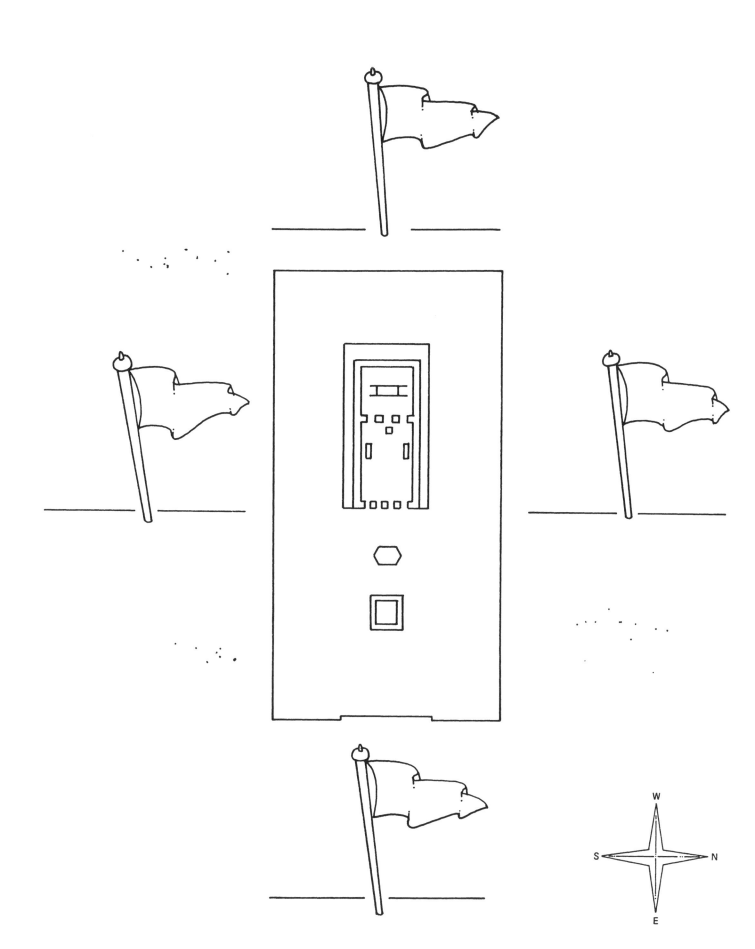

Exercises for Lessons 58 to 60

MAP WORK

1. Print Mt. Sinai next to the ◇ .

2. Print Taberah next to the ☼ .

3. Print Hazeroth next to the ● .

4. Print Wilderness of Paran next to the ♦ .

5. The Israelites sent out _____ from Kadesh. Print Kadesh next to the ✇ .

6. With a brown pencil crayon, trace the journey of the Israelites from Mt. Sinai to Kadesh.

7. The spies searched the land of Canaan from Hebron in the south to Hamath in the north. Print Hebron next to the △ . Print Hamath at the top of the map and make an arrow pointing north.

8. Print Hormah next to the ○ .

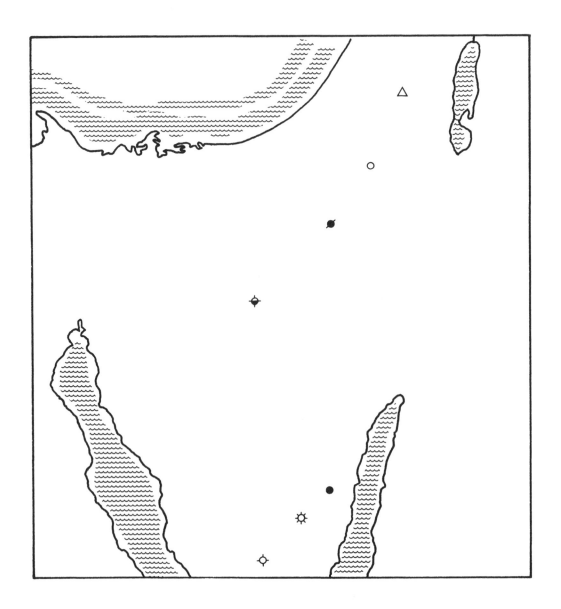

Near the end of Lesson 59, we read that God told Moses that the ungodly people in Israel had tempted Him ten times. You have followed the history of the Israelites closely, and will remember these ten times.

In each of these sentences which tell how Israel murmured against Jehovah, fill in the missing words. Remember: these are the evil words and deeds of the wicked men in Israel.

1. At the Red Sea they complained: "Were there no _____ in Egypt?" Exodus 14:11

2. At Marah they murmured: "What shall we _____ ?" Exodus 15:24

3. In the Wilderness of Sin they said: "Would we had died by the _____ _____ of Egypt." Exodus 16:3

4. In the wilderness, some of the people left manna until the next morning, and it bred _____ . Exodus 16:20.

5. In the wilderness, some of the people went out on the _____ day to gather manna. Exodus 16:27

6. At Rephidim they demanded: "Give us _____." Exodus 17:2

7. At Sinai the Lord told Moses: "They have made them a _____ , and have worshipped it." Exodus 32:8

8. At Taberah, "the people _____ ," and "the fire of the Lord consumed them that were in the _____ parts of the camp." Numbers 11:1

9. At Kibroth-hattaavah the Israelites remembered the fish, cucumbers, _____ , leeks, _____ and _____ of Egypt. Numbers 11:5

10. At Kadesh they said, "Let us make a _____ , and let us return into _____ ." Numbers 14:4

Exercises for Lessons 61 to 63

MAP WORK

For forty years the Israelites wandered in the Wilderness of Shur and the Wilderness of Paran.

1. Print Wilderness of Shur on the __ __ __ line.

   Print Wilderness of Paran on the _ _ _ _ _ line.

2. Print Kadesh next to the ◇ .

   Print Ezion-Geber next to the ☼ .

   Print Gulf of Akaba next to the ● .

   The Israelites wandered between these places you have just marked on your maps.

3. Print Dead Sea on the.......line.

   Print Jordan River alongside the river.

4. Print Mt. Hor next to the ○ .

   Print Edom next to the ✸ .

   Print Moab next to the ✶ .

   Print River Arnon next to the ◈ .

   Print Plains of Moab next to the ◗ .

   Print Canaan next to the ▲ .

5. In Lesson 63 we will learn that the Israelites had two choices: to march the easy way to Canaan, or to go the long, hard way around the country of Edom. God chose to have them go the hard way.

6. With your finger, trace the easy route from Kadesh northeast, under the Dead Sea, and then north toward the Jordan River, across the River Arnon, up to the Plains of Moab. This was not the way the Lord chose.

7. Now trace the hard way. Draw a line from Kadesh to Mt. Hor, then to Ezion-Geber. Make a curved line around the east side of Edom. We will go a bit ahead of Lesson 63 and draw a dotted line through Moab and over the River Arnon up to the Plains of Moab, where the Israelites camped before they crossed the Jordan River.

8. Color the wilderness light brown, and each of the other countries a different color. You may choose them. Color the bodies of water blue.

MAP WORK

On the map for Lessons 61 to 63, the land of Canaan looked very small. On this worksheet, Canaan is enlarged so that you can see and understand more details of the land.

Our last lessons stopped with the Israelites at the north boundary of Edom. This map will show in detail how the Israelites traveled to the Plain of Moab and were ready to cross the Jordan River.

1. Print Moab on the —— — line.

2. Print Midian on the_____line.

3. Print River Arnon next to the ◇ . This river was the north border of Moab.

4. Print Ammon on the •••• line. Moab and Ammon were the descendants of _____ .

5. You can see that the Ammonites lived far to the east of the Jordan River. Why? Because the Amorites, a powerful nation, came and conquered part of their land. They took part of the land of Moab, too.

6. Print Amorites on the—·——·—line.

7. Print Heshbon next to the ☼ .

8. Now we are ready to trace the journey of the Israelites. Starting at the bottom of the map, draw a line around the east side of Moab, across the River Arnon on the west side of Ammon, to Heshbon.

9. Far to the north is the land of Bashan. Print Bashan next to the ● .

10. Print Edrei, the name of the capital city, next to the ○ . Now draw a dotted line from Heshbon to Edrei.

11. Print Jordan River next to the ✦ .

12. Print Canaan next to the ✸ .

13. Print Plain of Moab next to the ✦ , and draw a line from Edrei to the Plain of Moab. Study your map to see the long, round-about way the Lord took His people to the gateway of Canaan.

14. In the top right-hand corner of your map draw an arrow pointing northeast. Balaam probably lived in that direction.

15. Print Jericho next to the ▰ . We will get to Jericho in our lessons next week.

Color each country, Moab, Midian, Ammon, and the land of the Amorites a pastel color. Color the bodies of water blue, and the rest of the territory tan.

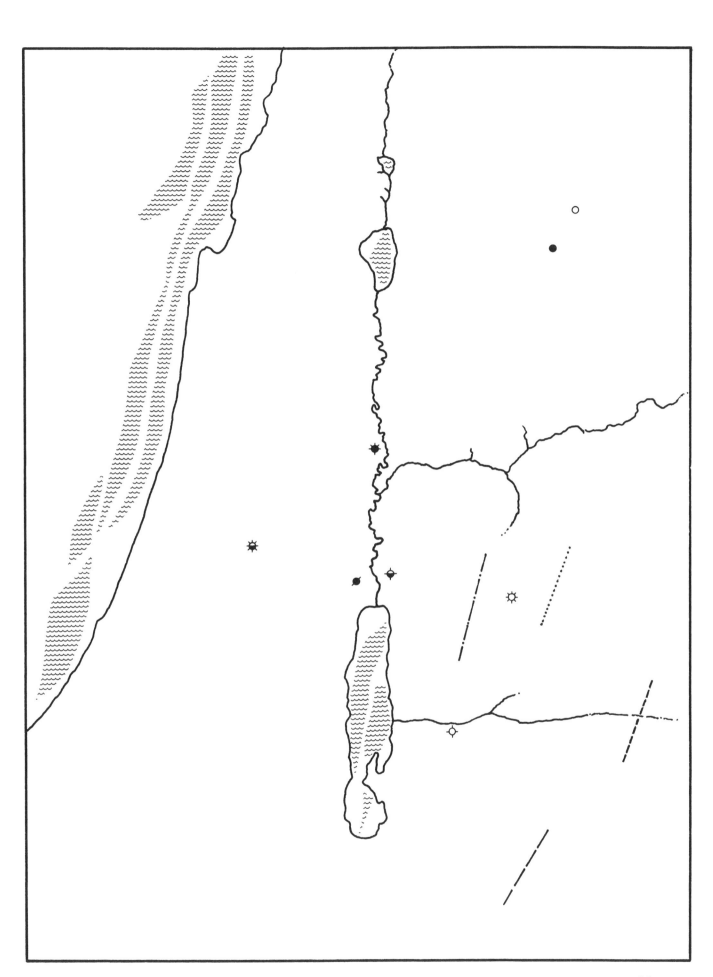

Exercises for Lessons 67 to 69

You are learning to look at many things in the Old Testament as types of things in the New Testament. In your lessons this week, you often compared Joshua with Jesus, because Joshua was a type of Jesus. On this worksheet, you will answer some questions about Joshua and Jesus.

1. Both the name Joshua and Jesus mean _____ .

2. Both Joshua and Jesus were captains of God's host, and they fought God's battles. But their weapons were entirely different. In your own words, tell what kinds of battles Joshua fought.
_____

   When Jesus came to earth, He fought, too, but not with weapons of war. What kind of battle did Jesus fight? _____

3. Before Joshua went into Canaan to fight, Jehovah made him strong and of good courage. Why did he need extra strength and courage from God? _____
_____

   Jesus needed strength and courage from His Father, too, when He was on earth. At what time in His life do you think Jesus needed a special measure of strength from His Father?_____
_____

4. Both Joshua and Jesus won great victories. Each won a special land. What land did God give Joshua and his people? _____ What land does God give Jesus and His people? _____

5. Both Joshua and Jesus came for judgment. The city of Jericho was ready for God's judgment when Joshua conquered it.

   Jesus is coming for judgment, too. When will He come? _____
Whom will He judge?_____

IDEA CORNER
   Sing Psalter number 213, stanzas 2 and 3, in class. This song is taken from Psalm 87.

WORD MATCHING

These stone pillars will test your memory. Each stone on one side of the river has a word which we studied these six weeks. Each stone on the other side of the river has a word meaning on it.

With your pencil crayons, match the colors of each word and its meaning, coloring lightly. For example, if you color the cleft stone brown, color the answer stone brown also. Use twelve different colors.

MAP WORK

You have only a small map of the southern part of Canaan this week. This is the area of Canaan where Joshua and the Israelites fought their enemies.

1. Print Ai next to the ✧ .

2. Print Bethel next to the ☼ .

3. Print Mt. Ebal next to the ● .

4. Print Mt. Gerizim next to the ○ .

5. Which was the mount of blessing? _____

6. Print Gibeon next to the ✦ .

7. Did the Gibeonites fight against Israel? _____

8. Print Gilgal next to the ✳ . This Gilgal was not the same Gilgal as the city near the Jordan River where the Israelites celebrated the passover.

9. In next week's lesson, you will meet the five kings of the south who came to fight Joshua and Israel. Find their cities:

    a. Print Jerusalem next to the ✪ .   b. Print Hebron next to the ◆ .

    c. Print Jarmuth next to the ▲ .   d. Print Lachish next to the ⚬ .

    e. Print Eglon next to the ☐ .

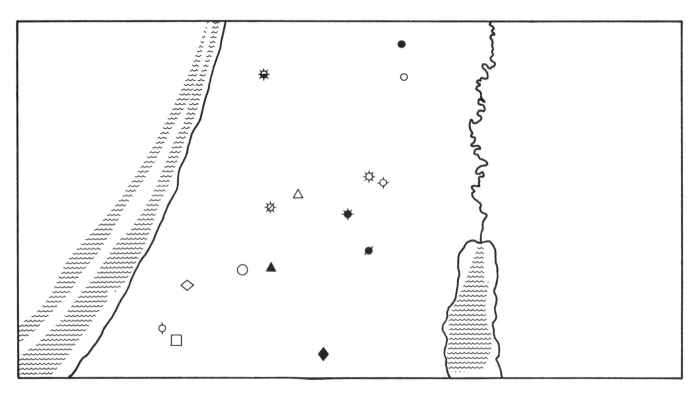

1. Very often we read in the Bible about the tribes of the people who lived in Canaan. We have met them in Lesson 72. They were all descendants of the grandson of Noah who was cursed by God. What was his name? _____

2. These seven tribes were sometimes lumped together and called Canaanites. All the names of the tribes ended in ite. Find the names in Joshua 3:10 and write them on these lines.

_____   _____   _____

_____   _____   _____

_____

3. In Acts 13, Paul talked about these seven nations of Canaan in one of his sermons. Read verses 14 to 20. In what city was Paul preaching? _____ Copy the verse which mentions the seven nations of Canaan. _____

_____

_____

4. In God's eternal plan, Rahab, who was saved from Jericho, had a very important place. Find Matthew 1:1 in your Bibles and read it. The generations of Jesus means His ancestors. Notice in verse 2 that we know the ancestors mentioned there. Now read verse 5. Rahab's name is spelled a little differently in the King James Version. On the lines below, write why it was very important that Rahab's life was saved. _____

_____

_____

_____

IDEA CORNER

On a separate sheet of paper, draw a sketch of the battle of Ai. Start with an x for Ai. Put Bethel two miles west. Show the ambush of 5,000 soldiers on the west of Ai. Show the main army of 30,000 on the north. Show Joshua between the two armies, where both could see his rod. Use words or pictures to show the battle positions.

Make Psalter number 121 (Psalm 44) stanzas 1, 2, and 4 your theme song for the week.

Exercises for Lessons 73 to 75

MAP WORK

Part 1. First, on last week's map, you will print the names of these cities:

Print Beth-horon next to the △ .

Print Azekah next to the ○ .

Print Makkedah next to the ◇ .

Now make a line tracing the long distance Israel pursued their enemies: from Gibeon to Beth-horon to Azekah to Makkedah.

Part 2. Print Ajalon next to the ☼ . Put an X between Gibeon and Ajalon.

Use the map on the opposite page.

Part 3. In Israel's battle with the tribes of the north, we met these places:

Print Sea of Chinnereth next to the ⬙ .

Print Mt. Hermon next to the ☼ .

Print Waters of Merom next to the ● .

Print Hazor next to the ☿ .

Part 4. To help you understand where Jehovah gave each tribe its inheritance, your map has heavy boundary lines on it. Print the name of each tribe inside these boundary lines. Remember, two and one half tribes lived on the east side of the Jordan. We will label those first.

a. Print Reuben next to the ✦ .

b. Print Gad next to the ✹ .

c. Print Manasseh next to the ◆ . You will print Manasseh once more, because the other half tribe lived on the west side of the Jordan River.

Starting at the southern part of Canaan, locate the rest of the tribes.

d. Print Simeon next to the ✎ .

e. Print Judah next to the ⬠ .

f. Print Benjamin next to the ✧ .

g. Print Dan next to the ☻ .

h. Print Ephraim next to the ☼ .

i. Print Manasseh next to the ◆ .

j. Print Issachar next to the ✦ .

k. Print Zebulon next to the ◆ .

l. Print Naphtali next to the ▲ .

m. Print Asher next to the ⬥ .

Before you study Lesson 75, find the cities of refuge:

a. Print Hebron next to the ◖ .

b. Print Shechem next to the ▬ .

c. Print Kedesh next to the ◖ .

d. Print Golan next to the ◀▶ .

e. Print Ramoth-Gilead next to the ♠ .

f. Print Bezer next to the ◗ .

Color each tribe's land a different color. The two parts of Manasseh's inheritance should be the same color.

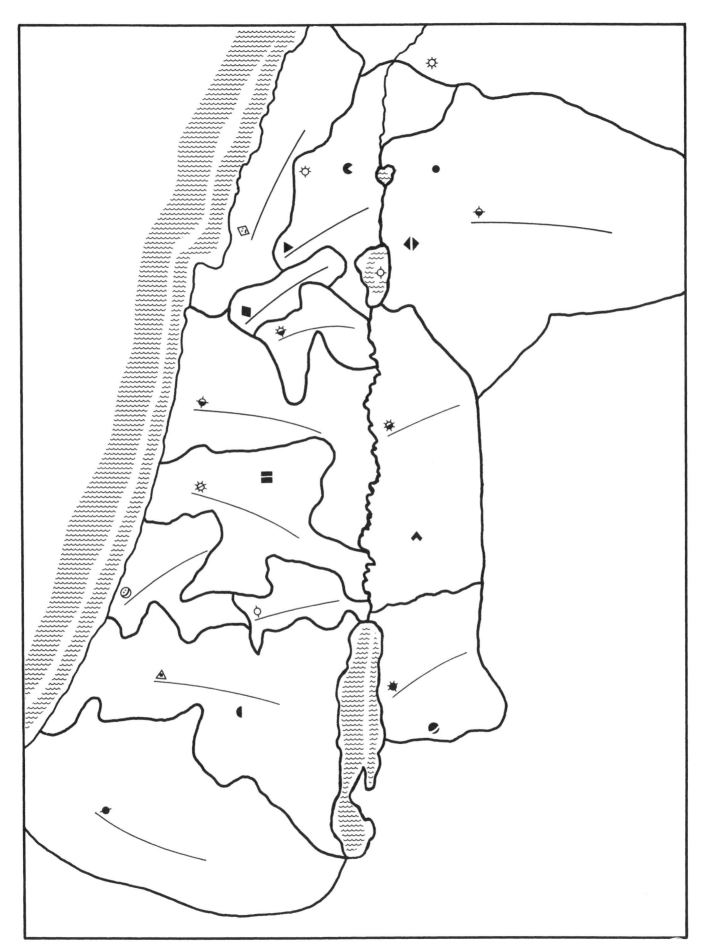

This is a vertical time line of the judges. First there are two dates, the years during which each judge ruled. No one is absolutely sure that these dates are accurate, but students of the Bible have figured the dates according to the information God gave them in the Bible. You will also notice that the number of the dates get smaller as time goes on. When time goes on and you grow older, the dates of your birthdays get higher.

The answer to this problem is that in the Old Testament, time is counted backward, starting at the birth of Christ. His birth is counted as zero, and we count time by figuring out how many years before Christ something happened. The period of the judges runs from about 1400 to 1060 before Christ (B.C.).

In the time line, some years are skipped. It means that there was no judge at this time. Samuel did not die during the period of the judges, but lived during the reign of Israel's first king.

As you study the judges, you will be asked to memorize them in order. Where the line of the judges separates, learn those in the left column first, and then those in the right column. These judges ruled at the same time, in different parts of the country.

1405 to 1367 — Joshua and the elders

1360 to 1321 — Othniel

1304 to 1225 — Ehud (also Shamgar)

1206 to 1167 — Deborah and Barak

1161 to 1122 — Gideon (also Abimelech, Tola, Jair)

1105 to 1100 — Jephthah

1100 to 1094 — Ibzan

1102 to 1083 — Samson

1094 to 1085 — Elon

1119 to 1080 — Eli

1085 to 1078 — Abdon

1100 . . . . — Samuel

MAP WORK

On this map you will find some of the places we have met before the time of the first judges of Israel.

1. Print Shechem next to the ✧ . Whose bones were buried there? _____

These are the places you met in the story of Micah in Lesson 77.

2. Print Mt. Ephraim on the _ _ _ _ line. Who lived there? _____

3. Print Zorah next to the ☼ and Eshtaol next to the ● .
   These two cities were in the land of the tribe of _____ .

4. Print Laish next to the ✸ . What did the soldiers who conquered Laish name the city?

_____

These are the places you met in the story of the Levite in Lesson 78.

5. Print Bethlehem next to the ✸ . The Levite went there to get his _____ .

6. Print Gibeah next to the ✦ . Gibeah was in the land of the tribe of _____ .

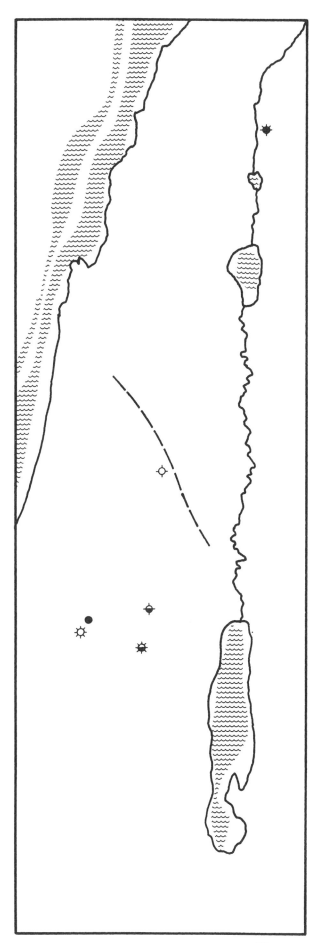

52

Exercises for Lessons 79 to 81

MAP WORK

At the end of Lesson 79 (and in Judges 21:19-21) we read about Shiloh. What happened at Shiloh every year? _____

_____

1. What did the men of Benjamin do at Shiloh? _____

_____

2. Print Shiloh next to the ✧ .

In Lesson 80 we met these places:

1. Print Moab next to the ☼ .   2. Print Ammon next to the ✹ .

3. Print Amalek next to the ● .   4. Print Jericho next to the ✺ .

5. Print Gilgal next to the ○ .

In Lesson 81 we met Barak from Kedesh in Naphtali.

1. Print Kedesh next to the ✦ .   2. Print Naphtali next to the ☐ .

3. Print Benjamin next to the ✒ .   4. Print Ephraim next to the ■ .

5. Print Zebulon next to the ▲ .   6. Print Ramah next to the ◆ .

7. Print Bethel next to the △ .   8. Print Kishon next to the ◇ .

Who judged between Ramah and Bethel? _____

9. Print Mt. Tabor next to the ☼ .   10. Print Megiddo next to the ◐ .

Tell in your own words why the Lord put the words of Judges 5:24 into Deborah's mouth.

_____

_____

_____

IDEA CORNER

Read the Song of Deborah at your devotions at lunch time.

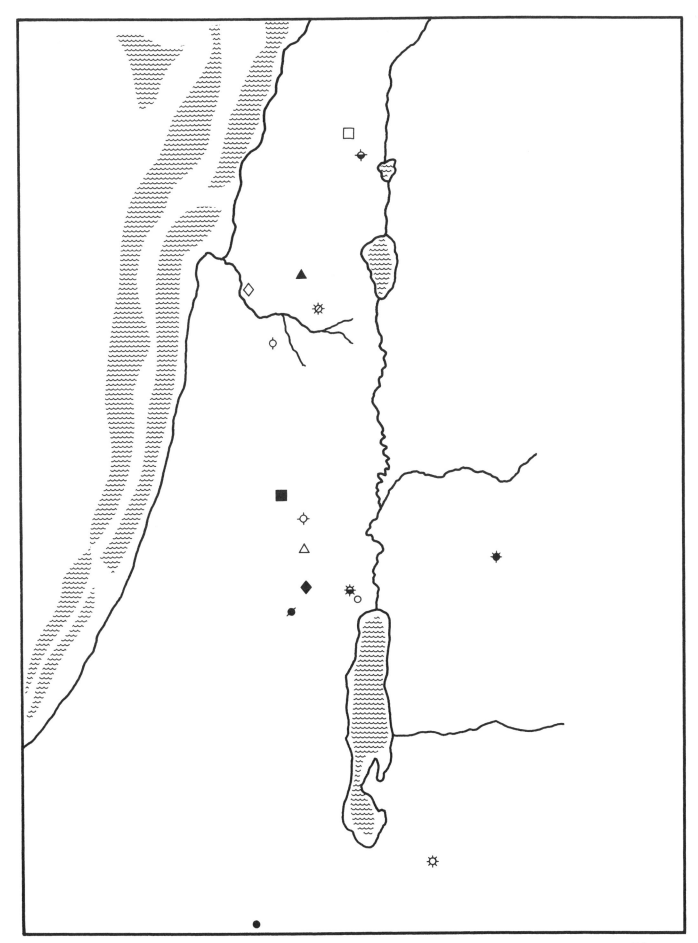

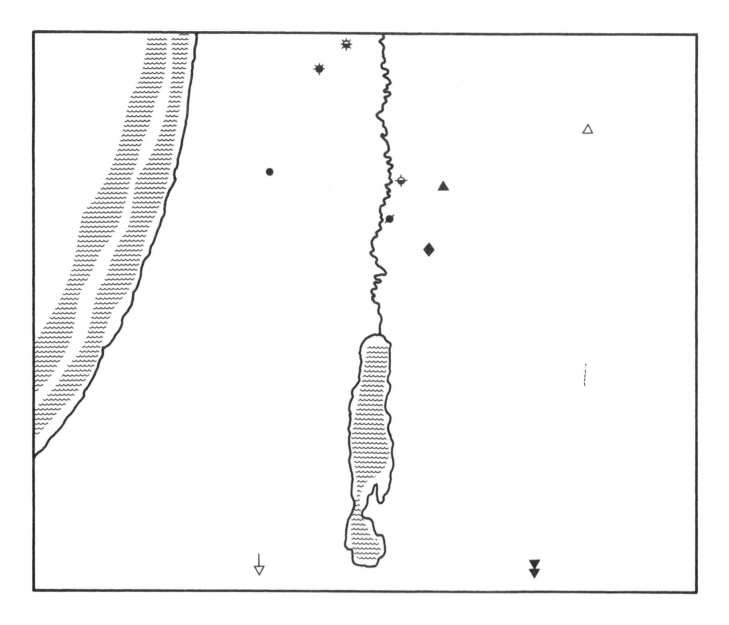

MAP WORK

1. Print Midian next to the ⬇⬇ .

2. Midian asked Amalek to help them oppress Israel. Print Amalek next to the ⬇ . You have found these places before, but this is a good review.

3. Print Ophrah next to the ● .   4. Print Jezreel next to the ✳ .

5. Print Hill of Moreh next to the ✴ .   6. Print Beth-Barah next to the ⬦ .

7. Print Succoth next to the ⬤ , and Penuel next to the ▲ . What happened at these two cities? _____

8. Print Karkor next to the △ .

9. Print Mizpeh next to the ◆ . We will meet Mizpeh in Lesson 86.

We have learned in earlier lessons that God has created many things in our world to be types of heavenly realities. Gideon knew from God's Word that dew is a type of God's blessings on His people. We studied it in Lesson 82, in the sign that Gideon asked of the Lord.

1. Find Genesis 27:28, and copy it on these lines. _____

_____

_____

To whom did God promise blessings, as dew, in this verse? _____

2. Find Deuteronomy 33:13 and copy it on these lines. _____

_____

_____

To whom did God promise blessings in this verse? _____

3. In Lesson 83, Israel learned that the sword of the Word of Jehovah won the battle. That sword and that Word are ours, too. Paul tells us about it in Ephesians 6:17. Copy it on these lines. _____

_____

Think of one way you can use the sword of the Spirit, which is the Word of God, in your life.

_____

_____

4. In Lesson 84 we learned that it was Jehovah Who defended Israel. Many years later the poet Asaph wrote Psalm 83, which was a Prayer for Israel's Defense. Copy verse 11 on these lines.

_____

_____

In the last verse of the psalm, Asaph tells us the reason he wrote Psalm 83. In your own words, tell why he wrote it. _____

_____

_____

IDEA CORNER

Psalter number 224 is a song from Asaph's psalm. Sing it, and make stanza 4 your theme song for the week.

Exercises for Lessons 85 to 87

Lesson 85.

1. The mother of Abimelech was a descendant of Shechem, the son of Hamor, whom we met in Jacob's time. Find Genesis 34:3. Whom did Shechem want to marry? _____ , the daughter of _____ . Already at that time, these Hivites wanted to join with Israel. How? (verse 9) _____

_____

2. Jotham told his fable from the mountains near Shechem. Two events took place at Shechem earlier in Bible history.

    a. Genesis 35:4 tells us that Jacob's family buried their _____ at an oak tree near Shechem on their way to _____ .

    b. Whom did Joshua gather together at Shechem? (Joshua 24:1) _____

_____

    c. In Shechem, Joshua also made a _____ with the people. (verse 25)

3. Jotham stood on Mt. Gerizim when he told the fable to Abimelech. In Lesson 71 we learned that six tribes of the Israelites stood on Mt. Gerizim. Which tribes were they?

_____ _____ _____

_____ _____ _____

4. In His law, God said that in the fourth year the fruits of the land shall be_____ _____ . The men of Shechem offered their crops to _____ .(Judges 9:27)

In Lessons 86 and 87 we saw the differences between the proud and the humble.

1. In Psalm 149:4, God uses another name for humble. It is _____ . How will Jehovah make the meek beautiful? _____

2. Solomon tells us, in Proverbs 16:18, that pride leads to _____ .

For our word review from our last six weeks' lessons, we will take a fig tree from Jotham's fable. You will find definitions on each side of the trunk. The answers are on the figs of the tree. Match the number of the definitions with the answers on the fruit. Put the number in front of each answer on the tree.

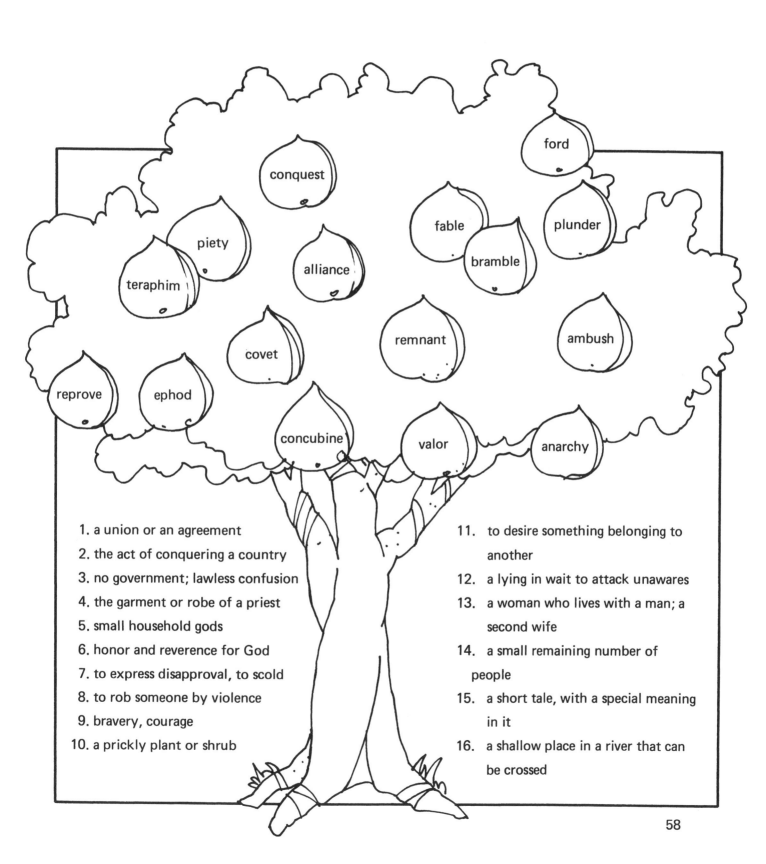

1. a union or an agreement
2. the act of conquering a country
3. no government; lawless confusion
4. the garment or robe of a priest
5. small household gods
6. honor and reverence for God
7. to express disapproval, to scold
8. to rob someone by violence
9. bravery, courage
10. a prickly plant or shrub

11. to desire something belonging to another
12. a lying in wait to attack unawares
13. a woman who lives with a man; a second wife
14. a small remaining number of people
15. a short tale, with a special meaning in it
16. a shallow place in a river that can be crossed

Exercises for Lessons 88 to 90

MAP WORK

From Lesson 88:

1. On the small map below, find the land of the Philistines. Print Philistines sideways through the land.

2. Print Zorah next to the ◇ . In which tribe was the city of Zorah? _____
Chapter 13:2 tells us who lived in Zorah _____ .

From Lesson 89:

1. At the beginning of Lesson 89, you learned that the Spirit of Jehovah moved Samson between Zorah and Eshtaol. Print Eshtaol next to the ☼ .

2. From there Samson went to Timnath. Print Timnath next to the ● .

3. After his wife told the Philistines the answer to his riddle, Samson went to Ashkelon. Print Ashkelon next to the ○ . What did Samson do in Ashkelon? _____

From Lesson 90:

1. Print Etam next to the ✦ .

2. Print Lehi next to the ✳ . The Philistines went to Lehi to fight _____ .
The rock Etam was close to Lehi.

3. Print Gaza next to the ✦ . What did Samson do at Gaza? _____
_____

4. Print Sorek next to the ⬤ . Who lived in Sorek? _____

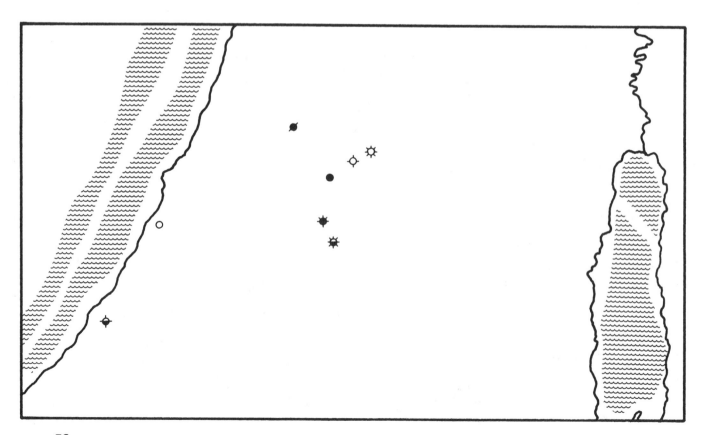

1. In Lesson 88 we learned about Nazarites. The Bible mentions only two other men who were Nazarites all their lives. They were _____ and _____ .

    a. Nazarites were Old Testament types. Jesus came to fulfill the types.

    b. Nazarites might not eat _____ nor drink _____ .

    c. Jesus Christ came _____ and _____ , Matthew 11:19.

    d. Wine is a picture of Jesus' blessings. Jesus told His disciples: "I am the _____ and ye are the _____ ," John 15:5.

    e. Jesus promised us that we shall eat of the fruit of the vine in His Father's kingdom, Matthew 26:29. When will that be? _____

2. The Bible has many sayings which we use in our everyday life.

    a. In Lesson 89 we learned that "plow with my heifer" means _____
_____

    b. In your own words tell what you think these words of Ahab mean: "Let not him that girdeth on his harness boast himself as he that putteth it off," I Kings 20:11. (Harness in this verse means armor for battle.) _____
_____
_____

3. In Lesson 90 we learned that the men of Judah were traitors. They gave Samson, bound and helpless, to the Philistines. Think of the greatest traitor in Bible history: _____
Whom did he betray? _____

4. Jehovah gave Samson water from the rock. Samson drank real water from the rock. At the same time, he drank spiritual water, for when he drank it, Jehovah taught Samson to trust in Him. Who else drank from the rock, Exodus 17:6? _____

    I Corinthians 10:4 tells us Who that rock was: _____

Exercises for Lessons 91 to 93

From Lesson 91:

1. Once more, read Ruth 1:16. These words of Ruth live in our hearts, too. On the lines below, write why you want to go to, live with, to die, and be buried with God's people. _____

_____

_____

2. In verse 20, Naomi asked to be called Marah, which means _____ .
In an earlier lesson, we have traveled with Israel to a place called Marah. What happened there? (See Lesson 48.) _____

_____

_____

3. Chapter 2:4 shows us how much God was in the thoughts of Boaz and his servants. What do you think about greeting your friends this way? _____

_____

_____

From Lesson 92:

4. God's people in Israel understood that the harvest of their crops was a type of God's blessings. Hosea 10:12 explains to us the meaning of sowing and reaping. Read it and explain three things:

    a. how you can plant righteousness _____

_____

    b. how you can harvest mercy _____

_____

    c. how God rains righteousness on you _____

_____

5. Have you memorized the names of the judges in order? We have finished our study of the period of the judges.

IDEA CORNER

    Sing Psalter number 357:3, 4 (Psalm 126). It is a song of harvest.

From Lesson 93:

This simple chart will give you an idea of the three large periods of Old Testament history, and it will show you how far in Israel's history we have studied this year. We are about 260 years into the third period, at the x.

1. From the promise in Genesis 3:15 to the flood was about 1656 years. Print to the flood on the line under this bar.
2. From the flood to the conquest of Canaan was about 1,000 years. Print to the conquest of Canaan under this bar.
3. From the conquest of Canaan to the birth of Christ was about 1,350 years. Print to Christ under this bar.

These dates are not certain, but the Bible gives us enough dates to give us a fairly accurate understanding of the periods of the Old Testament.

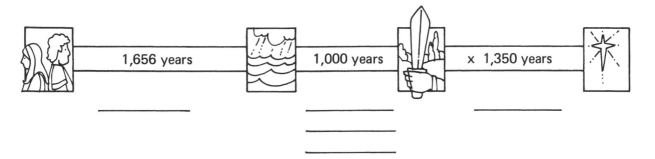

1,656 years   1,000 years   x 1,350 years

_____   _____   _____

                     _____

                     _____

The Song of Hannah is written for us in I Samuel 2:1-10. Hannah's prayer teaches us how to pray.

a. In verses 2 and 3, she describes God in three different ways. She describes Him in two ways in verse 2: as _____ , and as a _____ . In verse 3, she calls Him a God of

_____

b. In much of the song, Hannah sings about opposites. Find three opposites in her song, from verses 5 through 7, and write them on the lines. _____

_____   _____

c. The whole song tells the difference between God's children and God's enemies. Read verse 9. Can you think of another sharp opposite between God's people and the wicked? _____

Exercises for Lessons 94 to 96

Mapwork for two of our earlier lessons

Lesson 91

1. Print Bethlehem next to the ✧ . It was the home of _____ and _____ .
Ephrath was the name of the country surrounding Bethlehem. Print Ephrath next to the ⌢ .

2. Print Moab next to the ☼ . Trace their trip from Ephrath (near Bethlehem) to Moab.

Lesson 93

Print Ramah next to the ● .

Mapwork for this week's lessons

Lesson 95

1. In the battle in which the Philistines stole the ark, they were gathered at Aphek. Print Aphek next to the ✿ .

2. Print Ebenezer next to the ○ . Who camped at Ebenezer? _____

3. Print Ashdod next to the ✦ , Gath next to the ✹ , Ekron next to the ✦ . What traveled to these three cities? _____ Trace the route it took.

Lesson 96

1. Print Beth-shemesh next to the ✿ .

2. The ark went to Kirjath-jearim. Print ark next to the ✧ . Print Mizpeh next to the ✿ .

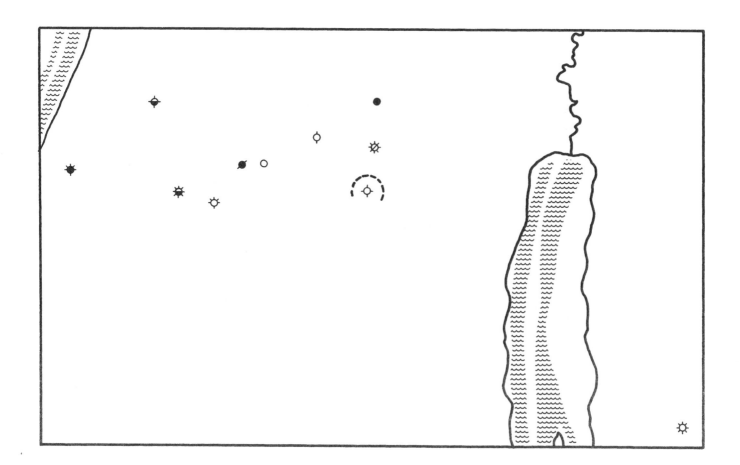

63

In Lesson 94 we studied obedience and disobedience. On our worksheet you will discover God's Words about these two opposites.

In Genesis 18:19, God blessed Abraham for his obedience.

In I Samuel 2:29, God spoke judgment to Eli because of his disobedience.

Remember, both these men were children of God. Now read these two verses and tell in your own words on the lines below the differences in these two families. _____

_____

God speaks to children, too, about obedience. Find Ephesians 6:1, and copy it on these lines. Then memorize it. _____

_____

In Lesson 95 the Philistines defended their idol Dagon. That was foolish and it was unbelief. In Psalm 115:4-7 Jehovah describes idols. Read the verses, and in your own words describe what the idols cannot do. _____

_____

In Lesson 96 you learned that the Israelites poured out water (I Samuel 7:6). Lamentations 2:19 explains it. Write the first part of the verse, to the word Lord, on these lines. _____

_____

Can you give an example of pouring out your heart before the Lord? _____

_____

IDEA CORNER

Especially in connection with Lesson 95, a lesson about idol-worship, sing Psalter number 308 stanzas 2 and 4 (Psalm 115).

Also find the hymn, "Come, Thou Fount of Every Blessing," and sing stanza 2.

Find pictures of idols in encyclopedias or history books, and look at them with one purpose: to see how evil they are.

MAP WORK

Lesson 97

1. Samuel judged Israel in the southern part of Canaan, and traveled a circuit.

Print Bethel next to the ✧ .   Print Gilgal next to the ● .

Print Mizpeh next to the ☼ .   Print Ramah next to the ✧ .

Draw a line connecting these cities, and notice that they make a sort of circle.

2. The home of Saul, the first king of Israel, was in Gibeah, in the tribe of Benjamin.

Print Gibeah next to the ○ .   Print Mt. Ephraim next to the ☼ .

Print Shalisha next to the ✦ .

Why did Saul travel to these places? _____

Lesson 98

3. One of the signs which Samuel gave to Saul was that he would meet two men at Rachel's grave. Matthew 2:18 tells us it was at _____ .

4. From Bethlehem, Saul went to his home town of Gibeah. Who were stationed at Gibeah?

_____

Print Jabesh-Gilead next to the ✦ . What did the Ammonites threaten to do to the men of the city? _____

Lesson 99

5. In this lesson we learned the battle positions of the Philistines and the Israelites, chapter 13:2 and 3. Next to the word Gibeah on your map, put the number of soldiers who were with Jonathan.

Print Michmash next to the ✪ . How many soldiers did Saul have there? Print the number next to the word Michmash.

Print Geba next to the ☼ . Who were stationed there?_____ Notice how close these armies were stationed.

Print the number of soldiers Saul had left next to the word Gilgal.

IDEA CORNER

Read chapter 10:5. Then look up the names of these instruments in a Bible dictionary and a Bible encyclopedia. If you can find pictures of them, try to draw one or two on a separate sheet of paper.

For devotions, read Psalm 118:1-17.

Sing Psalter number 317, taken from Psalm 118. Memorize stanza 3.

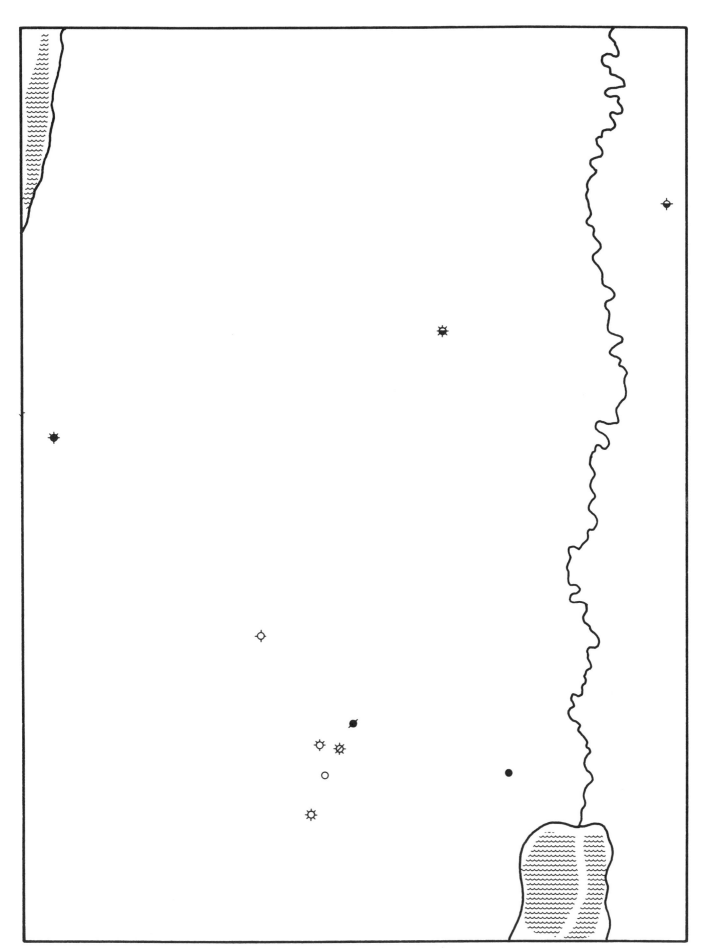

Exercises for Lessons 100 to 102

Word Studies Review

Because you have been studying Israel's first two kings, you will match crown words with scepter definitions in this vocabulary test. Draw lines from the crowns to the matching scepters.

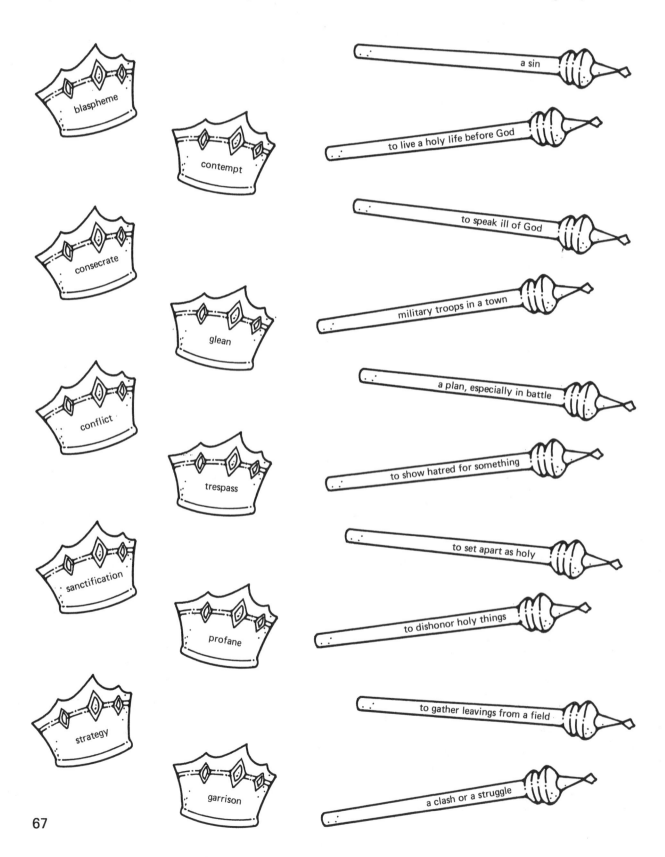

- blaspheme
- contempt
- consecrate
- glean
- conflict
- trespass
- sanctification
- profane
- strategy
- garrison

- a sin
- to live a holy life before God
- to speak ill of God
- military troops in a town
- a plan, especially in battle
- to show hatred for something
- to set apart as holy
- to dishonor holy things
- to gather leavings from a field
- a clash or a struggle

MAP WORK

On the small map below, you will follow Saul's route in his battle with the Amalekites.

1. Print Telaim next to the ♢ . What did Saul do at Telaim? (Lesson 101) _____

_____

2. Print Amalekites on the dotted line.

3. Print Carmel next to the ☼ . What did Saul do there? _____

_____

4. Print Gilgal next to the ● . Who met Saul at Gilgal? _____

5. Print Bethlehem next to the ○ . Name two things Samuel did at Bethlehem.

_____   _____

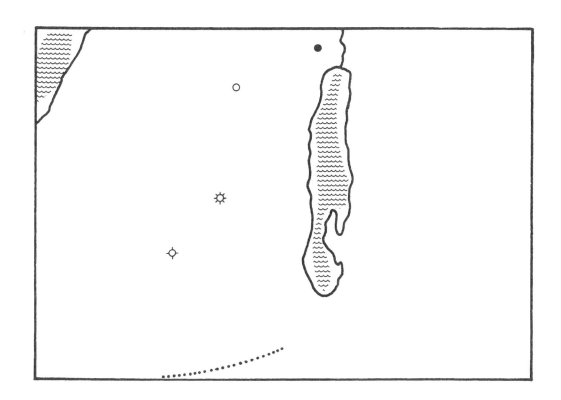

Read I Samuel 15:22.

The prophet Isaiah **tells us more about** sacrifices without repentance **and** obedience with repentance.

Read Isaiah 1:11 and 15. In your own words, tell what the Lord thinks of sacrifices without repentance. _____

_____

Read verses 16-18. In your own words tell what the Lord wants us to do in obedience.

_____

IDEA CORNER

Sing the song, "Though Your Sins Be As Scarlet."